mindgames

SimonHall

a
SUbtle
publication

Scripture Union

For Pete and Sam, who opened my mind to new things from God

SUbtle products are youth publications of
Scripture Union, 207–209 Queensway, Bletchley, MK2 2EB, England.

© Simon Hall 1998

ISBN 1 85999 281 1

British Library Cataloguing-in-Publication Data
A catalogue record for this book is available from the British Library.

Cover design by Sue Jackson and Darren Hill.

Printed and bound in Great Britain by Ebenezer Baylis & Son Limited, The Trinity Press, Worcester and London.

CONTENTS

INTRODUCTION

Welcome to *Mind Games*. This book is particularly for you, if you, or people you know, have ever sat in a church or house group and thought, 'There must be better ways of learning this.' *Mind Games* has been written for the millions of people who learn things more effectively through play, exploration, creativity and imagination. These people tend to be under-represented in the church because of its often rational, logical approach to God. To some of us, the idea that God can be reduced to a few doctrinal statements seems absurd. The Bible is central to their faith, but to many Christians it is the sound of waves on rocks, a week in silence in a hermit's cell, the music of a composer like John Taverner or even a night in a restaurant with friends which represents God most powerfully. These people are sitting in your church and house group week in, week out. They may seem to be the underachievers, the troublemakers, the ones who seem to deliberately fail to understand, those who never contribute. If you are one of these people, you may have felt as if Christianity just wasn't for you, or you may struggle with applying your faith to your everyday life.

According to scientists, this could be down to the way our brain works. The right side of our brain is the area that 'perceives' information which we're getting from all around us: sights, smells, tastes, etc. This is still a kind of raw experience until the left side of the brain gets to work on it, analysing and categorising it and trying to make it fit in with what we know already.

Apparently, we have a natural tendency to favour one side of the brain to the other and this results in some differences: scientists tend to be left-siders, trying to understand exactly what everything means, while artists tend to be right-siders, focusing more on the experience itself rather than on its interpretation. Within the church, theologians tend to be left-siders and mystics tend to be right-siders, although obviously there are exceptions to this rule. Whilst not technically correct, I am going to use shorthand throughout the rest of the book: instead of talking about right and left sides of the brain, I'm going to refer to our capacity for imagination and rationality.

In truth, we are all using both sides of our brains all the time, but most church teaching doesn't take that into account. We all need input that touches our imaginations as well as the rational part of our minds. Within my own church we have begun experimenting, using sights and sounds to help us in our prayer, and having testimonies, debates and discussions as well as sermons to help us learn and apply our learning.

The Bible is full of examples of how God teaches his followers through experiences that ignite their imaginations. God appeared to Moses and the Israelites in a number of powerful ways: a burning bush (Exodus 3), columns of smoke or fire (Exodus 13:21), a storm on Mount Sinai (Exodus 19:16–19); Ezekiel was asked by God to lie on his side in order to say something to Israel and Judah which they were obviously not going to hear or understand in any other way (Ezekiel 4:4–6); Hosea lived a prophetic life that none of us would wish to emulate (Hosea 1:1–11; 3:1–5); Jesus used miracles and parables to communicate truths about God. This is not to deny that huge tracts of the Bible are law, history or teaching, but is to restore balance to what has often been a purely rational expression of faith in the risen Lord Jesus. There are many Christians who have struggled over the years with a feeling that there must be more to God than the four spiritual laws.

If that's you, or you know friends or fellow church members who might identify with these issues, or if you're a leader wanting to expand your communication of the gospel, this book is for you. It outlines a number of ways in which you can help yourself or others to learn about or experience God. Each chapter explores a particular learning technique, suggesting how it could be used, giving some 'ready-to-use' examples and offering tips for developing your own variations on a theme.

Not all of the exercises relate directly to learning about God or the Bible, but I have provided relevant Bible references for most of them. As you will see, each method lends itself to learning about different aspects of life and faith, so some sections will have clearer biblical parallels than others. I have sorted all the exercises according to subject matter and you will find a simple index at the back. While the exercises are 'ready-to-use', very few will work well if you open this book five minutes before a meeting, looking for a quick fix. Take time to think about how you can fit your chosen learning experience into a group meeting.

If you are not part of a group that could use these exercises, look out for the ☺ symbol, which indicates an activity which can easily be used by, or adapted for, one person on their own.

Some of the methods of experiencing and learning carry a health warning, and at the end of each introductory section you will find general outlines on how to use these exercises safely. Some of the role-plays and meditations have the potential to open people up to feelings that they may have trouble dealing with on their own. They are not to be treated as mere games or 'ice-breakers': they are tried and tested learning tools which need to be handled accordingly.

Finally, those who are interested in these kinds of subjects will notice one glaring omission: my own feeling is that storytelling needs a separate book in its own right, not only because of the great biblical tradition of storytelling, but because anthropologists, sociologists, psychologists and therapists of every kind are telling us about the importance of storytelling for the well-being of both individuals and communities. You might like to read *Storytelling: a practical guide* by Lance Pierson (Scripture Union 1997), for some further ideas on this subject.

HOW DOES THIS BOOK WORK?

This is, above all, a practical book, the aim of which is to help you and those you love learn more about and experience God in new and deeper ways. After a brief warm-up ('Before we get going ...') each of the main chapters follows the same course. There's an introduction to a particular kind of learning method, including a basic explanation of what it's all about, followed by some general advice on how to use the exercises appropriately. There are then a number of exercises to use in whatever context you feel is right for you: all of them are designed to be used in a church, house group or youth group setting, but most of them can also be used on your own. After the examples, you will find a DIY section giving basic advice on how to create your own role-plays/meditations/ rituals, etc. If this book does well, *Mind Games II* will no doubt be published (tell your friends – ed). If you take the lessons of this book to heart and would like to contribute any of your ideas to a follow-up, you can contact me at:

204 King Lane
Leeds
LS17 6AA

or at:

revive@bigfoot.com

Thanks. And I hope God blows your mind!

Simon Hall
Pentecost 1998

BEFORE WE GET GOING ...

Here's a page of simple 'warm-up exercises' for groups that have never experimented with these kinds of activities before. They are based on resources especially designed for use in a small group (cell group) context. Divide folk up (if necessary) into groups of about 6 and get everyone to discuss one of these questions. Within a few weeks everyone will be ready to continue the adventure!

- Imagine you have arrived at the day of judgement and God says to you, 'In the new creation you are allowed to keep one thing only from the old order of the earth, and must destroy another.' What aspects of today's world would you want to see included and excluded from your vision of heaven?

- Who was your favourite teacher at school and why?

- Is your image of God more like your mum or dad, or someone else? Where do you get your image of God from?

- Where did you go on holiday when you were 8(ish)?

- If you had to choose between being beautiful and stupid, or ugly and clever, which would it be? Why?

- What one question would you like to ask God?

- If you were an animal, what kind of animal would you be? Why?

- What did/do you want to be when you grew/grow up?

- What would you like to be written on your epitaph?

- Would you rather be older or younger than you are? Why? Can you, as a group, suggest the age that society tells us we all want to be?

- What one dream would you like to fulfil in your lifetime?

1
CREATIVITY

DEFINITIONS

In the Bible, the first thing we learn about God is that he is a creative God. Before we know that he is good, righteous, merciful and loving, we know that he created the universe and said that it was good (Genesis 1:31). I deduce from this that creating gave God pleasure. One of the things that he made was us, and we were good too: particularly good, in fact, because we were made in God's image (v27). This chapter is about how we can continue to live in God's image in the area of creativity.

As you would expect, I cannot hope to cover how God can use our creativity in full so I am going to limit myself to the job in hand: helping people to learn about and experience God. There has been resistance to the use of art in some quarters of the church, but hopefully today we can ensure that people like Ernesto Lozada-Uzuriaga don't have to feel like outcasts.

Ernesto is a Peruvian refugee living in this country. He is also an artist and a Christian. When I first met him in about 1990, he was very much on the fringe of the church; but I could see that he was a brilliant artist, so I asked him to make some artwork for the church I was helping to lead at the time. Ernesto claims that despite growing up in the church, he had never before had the opportunity to use his artistic talent for God. The experience of painting for the church proved to be much more significant than either of us had imagined, and Ernesto was brought close to God through it. Today he helps to run the Bezalel Arts Trust, named after the person in the Bible who received special gifting in the area of art and crafts, from the Holy Spirit, in order to decorate the tabernacle (Exodus 31:2–5).

Artists have generally had a tough time in the church. Today we think of them as 'sensitive types' or even egomaniacs. The idea of someone dying for their art seems ludicrous to those of us who do not possess a gift in that area. Yet God died for us, his creations. Openness and honesty in putting something of yourself into your art brings a level of vulnerability that can lead to hurt and misunderstanding. We should not be too judgemental of the person who allows us to see into their soul. Some of these exercises will help us to encourage and accommodate the artist in our church. Like Ernesto, many practice their gift outside the church, not because they are in rebellion or because they feel the church is not good enough, but because no one in the church has tried to encourage or understand them. The blessings of a positive relationship with our artists is two-way.

SETTING

For many of us, the last time we did art in church was at Sunday School. We remember colouring pictures of Bible stories and – hey! – it only took 20 minutes. The main constraint on encouraging art is time. Trying to produce art in a hurry will produce certain kinds of results, not all of which will be bad, but will generally mean that we never get past Sunday School level. I'm a songwriter (of sorts) and I have written a few songs in an afternoon, but sometimes a song takes days or even weeks to come to fruition. The different exercises suggested here are based on a variety of time constraints, but generally they require either a gifted artist or time or both. It's important that there are exercises which allow everyone to contribute, but it is also important that some of the ideas are about giving honour to the creative talent (however embryonic) that we have in the church. Settings for exploring this area of creativity. therefore need to be thought through carefully. One or two of the ideas in this section are for public worship, but many others require time and space outside the constraints of a meeting that is really for something else.

The physical setting is really whatever is appropriate for the people or activity in hand. Church halls make great places to do art, music or dance workshops simply because there's so much space. However, taking people away to a new environment (townies to the country and vice versa) can prove a simple inspiration to creativity.

The main requirements for the sessions themselves are technical: the number of times I've had to run out mid-session to buy scissors or tape or something truly basic is embarrassing, so make sure you are equipped beforehand with any tools or equipment you may need. Also make sure there are enough to go around. There's nothing more frustrating than having to wait in turn for three other people to finish using the coloured markers or the sellotape when you're in the full flow of creative genius!

GUIDELINES

It's almost impossible to lay down general guidelines for the exercises, as they are so different. However, here are a few thoughts.

Always be clear about what you want to achieve. Some of these exercises require some artistic ability, others don't. Getting a house group or youth group to produce pictures in half an hour is unlikely to produce gallery-standard material (although you could talk to Damien Hirst about that...). If you want to produce something top quality then you will need to rely on people who can do that. Otherwise, just enjoy. The main themes in this section are worship and self-expression/exploration, the connecting thread being that we all need to be valued as we do both.

As I've mentioned already, plan well so that you can run around being encouraging rather than running around being stressed. As with more 'religious' acts of self-disclosure, like praying or giving testimony, people need to be coaxed and encouraged at first, until eventually they are confident. The handling of the fragile ego of the person contributing is the only dangerous aspect of this kind of exercise!

EXAMPLES

1. Picture stories (eg Matthew 20:1–16) ☺

Despite shying away from storytelling in this book, this simple exercise helps groups to 'gel' by giving people a simple way to share testimony. Give everyone a piece of paper and access to a variety of coloured pens. Then ask them to draw their life story. Try to get everyone to use pictures or a diagrammatic form rather than words. You may like to have a few examples done already such as: the 'temperature chart' which goes up and down with the joys and sadnesses of life, the spiral staircase or the 'free-form' collection of unconnected picture-memories. Each will tell the group about the person's personality as well as their history. One good way to develop from this is to get everyone into pairs to describe their pictures, and then have each person introduce their partner to the wider group on the basis of what they have just learned.

2. Community cross

In South America, churches will often have huge crosses decorated with the story of the local community and God's interaction with it, alongside pictures from Bible stories. John Bunyan Baptist Church in Cowley, Oxford, has a beautiful cross in the same tradition. Why not try something similar that could involve those who are not so artistically gifted? A simple weekend project would be to create a 'community cross' by sending out a team to take photographs of local sights and people, and then pasting them onto a simple cross made out of any material, by someone else involved. A bit of paint and decoration can give the composition an extra dimension. The project could include local historians, writers, journalists, etc, as well as a wide variety of church members. Make sure that you produce a written key to what you produce (somebody who enjoys expressing their creativity through writing may enjoy this part) and display the cross prominently: telling stories is a key way of defining and preserving community.

3 Live art worship (2 Samuel 6:12–22)

Your ability to try out this idea is possibly limited by your own church context, but there's nothing to stop you creating an appropriate context. It's simple: allow artists in your church to contribute to the worship *in real time,* during the services. If you have folk in your church who are gifted in arts that have a visual element – particularly painting, dance and mime – encourage them to 'lead' worship through their art. Within my own church, we have used painters on either side of the room where we meet, creating art on huge sheets or boards. Using dance and/or mime within worship has been harder for us as a younger church because dance in church has generally been very traditional and we have no role models. Simple paintings and movements can be helpful within a supporting and understanding environment, so make sure everyone knows what's happening.

4 Songwriting workshop

In many churches there is a wonderful spread of talent, but nobody who has the ability and/or confidence to write songs for specific use in their local worship context. Provided you have one person who can sing and one who can play an instrument (keyboard or guitar is normally best) and who has a few chords up their sleeve, I can almost guarantee that you would be able to write a song within a day. When I run a songwriting day (or weekend), I get together no more than ten people and spend some time focusing on God at the beginning of the day. We then spend a bit of time in quiet, asking God if there is anything he wants us to write a song about, and from that we pick a couple of themes and brainstorm lots of words and phrases which come to mind. Meanwhile, our musician(s) is putting together some chords that feel right for the theme, ie angry, happy, sad, bouncy, awe-struck. There is no way to dictate what happens next: it's basically a free-for-all! The job of the facilitator is to encourage and ensure that everybody is heard and the finished product is 'owned' by everyone involved.

5 Psalmistry (1 Chronicles 16:7–13) ☺

Writing, re-writing or even writing music for psalms is a good way to begin to explore creativity. If you have spent time individually or as a group studying some psalms, why not try to write your own? If that seems too difficult, an easier option is to re-write a psalm that you like, with more modern language and metaphors. If you have composers in the church, ask them to write accompaniments to your new words. Ta-da! You have your own new songs!

6 Let's do theology (Isaiah 1:18) ☺

I first learned this simple way of exploring faith from Pete Ward at Oxford Youthworks, but I suspect it goes way back. All that's needed for this exercise is paper and pens (preferably coloured) for everyone.

Ask everyone to take 10 minutes to draw the world and themselves in it. When the time is up, ask people to fit God into their picture. Be ready for lots of torn-up paper! When everyone is finished (don't give them too long), get them into groups of 4–5 to share what they've drawn. Round off the exercise by explaining that everyone has been 'doing' theology – thinking about God. Leave people with a question about how God did or didn't fit into their view of the world, and ask if this has any meaning for them in their day-to-day lives.

7 Soundtracks and backdrops (Exodus 31:2–11)

Many of the newest churches are very aware of the way the creative arts can affect our experience of church. Many churchgoers think that young people are deceived or even hypnotised by the images and music in pop videos and adverts. However, on closer inspection, these media play on the younger generation's cynical and suspicious awareness that 'the medium is the message' and encourage a playful attitude to our new multimedia environment. So the use of background music, slides, videos and computer-generated images will all become the norm in time.

You will be pleased to know that playing music as part of a worship service is exempt from copyright (reproducing words isn't though, so beware!). As I write I am planning our next church service to begin with the crucifixion scene from *Jesus of Nazareth* on a video screen backed by *Wonderwall* by Oasis (try it, you'll be surprised!). The first time I did the DIY prayer and worship exercise (see below) we shot two rolls of slide film and ended up with a wide variety of home-grown images which we projected onto drapes (well, sheets stuck to the ceiling with tape actually).

Creating an environment for a service can be a fun and creative process, involving all kinds of people. However, beware of spending too much time on the trimmings and forgetting the main content and focus!

8 DIY prayer and worship (Habakkuk 1:2–5) ☺

This exercise is brilliant at teaching people the value of giving something of themselves in worship. You will need a good selection of tapes or CDs (or musicians if you've got them) and lots of paper, scissors, glue, pens, paint, etc. You also need a long evening or afternoon: it could be used for a sleepover.

A week before this exercise, ask your group to bring copies of their favourite magazines (explain that you will be cutting them up). If any read a newspaper, ask them to save articles that strike them and to bring them along as well. You may need to buy some extra papers and magazines so that there are enough to go round.

At the start of the meeting, spend 10–15 minutes letting everyone have a good look at what you've got. Encourage them to notice anything that catches their eye (avoid page three!). Then have a short time of prayer, asking God to bring to mind the stories or images that you should focus on. Divide everyone up into groups of 4–5, each with a theme chosen after the reading and prayer. You may need to be proactive in getting people to pick themes: the last time I did this with a group of young people, the areas they felt passionate about ranged from Bosnia to Michael (REM) Stipe's spiritual condition; from the ozone layer to the problem pages of *Just Seventeen*.

Now hand out as large a piece of paper as you can manage (wallpaper is excellent) to each group. Draw their attention to the art resources you have available, and ask them to create something which expresses their thoughts and feelings to God about the subject they have chosen. They can draw, write, or just put some cut-out articles and pictures onto the paper. Encourage creativity, but explain that they only have an hour (or less if your group is likely to get bored). You may need to have some input, or you may like to get an artist in your church to add some creative flair to the process.

When the time is up, have a break! Then spend some time putting together your artwork with some music (sung or just to listen or dance to) and create a 'service'. The main focus of the service will be that each group explains their artwork and then everyone responds through prayer, music or ritual (see chapter 2). This obviously requires a lot of last-minute innovation to fit everything together, but you can probably prepare quite a bit in advance just by being aware of what music the people involved like, and what issues

they are likely to bring up.

The quality of art and presentation will no doubt vary, but be encouraging that God has welcomed everyone's prayer and worship.

 Study groups (Ecclesiastes 1:13,14)

Art appreciation can be a wonderful opportunity for learning. Whether it's a group of Christians going to see a thought-provoking film together and talking about it afterwards, or a deliberately planned book club, these can all be times of personal refreshment but also great opportunities for sharing faith with others. So much great literature and film is about the search for meaning or redemption, that within certain social groups this may be one of the best ways into evangelism.

DIY

All these exercises are variations on a few themes. (1) How can I create something which will bring glory to God and/or communicate my feelings about him? (2) How can I express something of the mystery of God through art? (3) How can I communicate with others about the things that matter to me and learn from them, using art? (4) How can I encourage the artist in my church to see that his/her gift has been given by God for his glory?

Coming up with creative answers to these questions will inevitably lead you into organising all sorts of brilliant activities for people to participate in. The first time I did the DIY prayer and worship session was with a group of youth workers in the Lake District. I had been asked to speak about alternative worship and decided that I wanted to help the people coming to understand the significance of creating your own environment and style of worship. I only had an afternoon, so I

worked out an exercise that would be relatively quick and easy. At the end of the day, some of the youth workers gave me a backhanded compliment: 'We didn't understand what you were going on about for the morning, but once we did the thing with cutting up newspapers, it all began to make sense.'

This chapter hasn't really covered the power of art and creativity in the communication of the gospel to those who have never heard or understood it. There has been some work on this; in fact it's probably fair to say that, generally, special evangelistic meetings are more media-aware than our other church services. Perhaps this is an indication that we do know how to use the media but that we are unsure about how appropriate it all is in church. If you are going to encourage the use of creative arts in your church, I would simply suggest that you make clear to everyone what your main aim and focus is in doing so. When there is clarity of vision, people can't help but get behind you.

2 RITUAL AND SACRAMENT

DEFINITIONS

'Ritual' and 'sacrament' are words filled with meaning, although most of us aren't too sure what those meanings are! We might hear of ritualistic churches which use lots of liturgy and 'smells and bells', or we read in the papers about 'satanic rituals', without ever being told what these rituals are. The dictionaries tend to define ritual as 'a procedure regularly followed', ie anything we do over and over again. Sacrament is a bit easier: we know about baptism and communion and maybe marriage. Again I looked to the dictionaries, which advised me that a sacrament was a set way of saying or doing something which is regarded as an outward and visible sign of inward and spiritual grace and which ensures a blessing. Oh dear! Finding a word for what I want to describe is so difficult!

When I receive communion, many, many things are happening. I am becoming part of an almost timeless and repeated great tradition, but I am also saying that *today* I want to receive Jesus. By re-enacting an ancient story I am affecting the universe *today*. My physical actions (such as eating and drinking) have spiritual causes and consequences. These kinds of thoughts – the idea that individually or corporately there are things we can do that help us to connect with God – are what I'm trying to get at when I use words like ritual and sacrament.

I don't know how you pray, but at various times in my life I've learned to pray in different ways. Right now I like to pray standing up, because it helps me feel that I'm ready and willing to do God's bidding. At another time in my life I used to spend a lot of time face-down on the floor, because I wanted to humble myself before my Lord. Nowadays, if I'm sitting in a chair in a prayer meeting, with my head bowed, it means I'm not really willing to engage with God that day: my body language tells the story. Over time, the way I pray has developed a sacramental edge to it: I believe that how I pray physically, affects how I pray in terms of my passion or humility or my willingness to continue praying when all seems lost. The idea that our bodies and our minds/spirits are intertwined shouldn't surprise us: Jesus used the same word to describe both healing and salvation: *soteria* or wholeness (Luke 7:36–50, Luke 17:11–19). Paul reminds us that our bodies are temples of the Holy Spirit (1 Corinthians 6:19–20), not just our minds.

So I have a sacramental understanding of life: I want what I do to mean something to God, and some things I do (like taking communion) mean an awful lot. When I decide to do something for a special reason, like a foot-washing for example, I would call that a ritual. For me, a ritual is a corporate or individual act where the sacramental meaning is explicitly drawn out. We know why we take communion, and we have certain ways of giving and receiving the bread and wine. This is a ritual. However, we can have new rituals which engage the modern mind in wonderful and imaginative ways.

SETTING

Sacraments and rituals can take place all over the place. I know of someone who prays for every person they sit next to on a bus or train. They then often feel like talking to them: the spiritual act leading into practical Christian living. When I think about ritual and sacrament I always think about Gothic 'high' churches, but isn't it time those of us from a wider church context started learning from each other? So why not try some of these ideas (or some of your own) in your church service, or in your house group or youth group. I would generally advise that these exercises work best when used as a response to some kind of input, whether that be teaching or as part of a time of worship. You will need to judge your own setting with regard to how much you explain what's going on and how much people need to be guided through what happens. With a more mature audience, you could use an exercise at the beginning of a meeting and then spend some time reflecting on how everyone felt doing it, possibly even repeating it later on after people have shared their various interpretations of the exercise.

GUIDELINES

There are no particular dangers with using rituals, but there are a number of issues to be aware of, not least the fact that these activities, particularly if repeated a few times, can become like a secret language if they are not explained properly. Although it can be tedious, always explain what's going on. Having said that, you don't need to give a running commentary on people's experiences – 'Oh yes, and this bit means that we are now closer to God because Mark 17:3 says...' Allow everyone room for God to speak to them directly through what they are doing, and for them to respond. It may be that some folk will want to pray or be prayed for, during or after one of these exercises, so be prepared for any eventuality.

Finally, be prepared to explain what you've done afterwards. If you try some of these activities in a wider church setting (as I have), it is possible that someone will feel there's something a bit 'dodgy' about what you're doing. I would suggest asking them what their understanding of communion is, and starting from there, because most people would see taking bread and wine as a place where the natural and supernatural overlap in some way.

EXAMPLES

1 Re-imagining Communion (Luke 22:7–23; 1 Corinthians 10)

As a starter, why not think about various ways of helping people to understand the sacrament of Communion? Here are a few examples:

- Have everyone come to church (or a church hall) and share Communion in small groups around a table. The bread and wine could be part of a bigger meal.
- Encourage everyone in your group to give pieces of bread to particular friends as a sign of commitment to or thanksgiving for them. (Make sure, however, that no one is left out or feeling unvalued during this exercise.)
- Share in the making of the bread as part of the service. Find a way to cook it quickly, either by microwave or in small rolls in an oven, while the rest of the service continues and then enjoy it together in Communion at the end. This helps people to remember that the bread is the 'fruit of our hands'.
- However you normally serve Communion, try it in a different way: different churches often emphasise a different element of the sacrament.

2 Anointing with oil (Psalm 23:5; Luke 7:36–50)

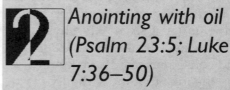

This is another traditional ritual which has recently found favour again. As well as anointing with oil (I tend to use cooking oil, but one summer holiday we were forced to use suntan oil), I pour water on people and blow on them as a sign of praying that God's Spirit will cover and fill them (Isaiah 44:3).

<footer>14</footer>

Foot-washing (John 13:1–17)

This works best within the context of a meeting which is looking at the issues this amazing act of Jesus brings up. Make sure you have a big bowl, some kind of plastic sheeting if you have a carpet, and a towel. Foot-washing was a symbol of a host's willingness to humble himself for his guests: perhaps you can think of a better modern alternative.

 ### Dirty hands (John 3:16,17; Philippians 2:1–13) ☺

We've used this simple concept in a couple of services where there has been a challenge to engage with the real world. People are invited to dig their hands into a bucket of earth as a sign of being willing to take on dealing with the muck in the world. Another interpretation is to celebrate that we are part of the earth.

 ### Good-bye to sin (Psalm 32; Psalm 103:12; 1 Corinthians 3:10–15) ☺

This simple ritual has been around for some time but it maintains its potency. Make a simple cross and place a metal bucket at its foot. Then give everyone a pen and a piece of paper, and ask them to write down any sins which they would like to give over to God for forgiveness. Ask them to put the folded papers in the bucket where they are lit and allowed to burn. The symbolism is fairly self-evident.

    Handy hint: keep a fire extinguisher handy!

 ### Dangerous worship (Luke 12:32–34; Romans 12:1,2)

Sometimes church worship services include lots of *words* about how our lives belong to God or how we are willing to do anything for him. Why not construct some form of altar and invite members of your group to *show* God and his people that they are willing to give up something for him as part of the meeting? (It's up to you whether you give people their car keys and credit cards back, and it's up to you whether you tell them in advance if they'll get them back or not!)

 ### IOU (Amos 5:14,15; Mark 10:17–23) ☺

If the above is too extreme, try this: get everyone to think of some area of their life or some possession which they have not brought under God's rule. Ask them to write an 'IOU' note to God, and collect these up or have people bring them to an altar.

 ### Dear me (Psalm 42; Psalm 104:1) ☺

This exercise works well if you have people away for a weekend or week. Take time towards the end of your meeting/holiday for everyone to write themselves a letter about what they have learned and what they want to do about it. They should put the letter in a self-addressed envelope and then hand them in to you. Explain that you will send them out after 3/6/12 months. It is always enlightening, challenging and/or amusing to get your letter back after you've (normally) forgotten what you'd learned.

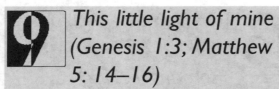

This little light of mine (Genesis 1:3; Matthew 5: 14–16)

Using candles is a very simple way of creating powerful imagery and ritual. So many 'high' churches continue to have special areas where people can light a candle as a way of saying a prayer and the final scene of Baz Luhrmann's film *Romeo and Juliet*, which shows an entire cathedral illuminated by thousands of candles, should be enough to remind us of the power of candles in the popular imagination. Use them to change the atmosphere of a room; dim or black out some light, use a big candle as a sign of Jesus' light and get everyone to light tapers from it; have people sharing the light around a room. Candles can be used in many different situations, so just be imaginative!

DIY

I have already indicated in the examples that there are numerous variations of every ritual you might come up with, which is great because it means you can always do something new. The main rule that I apply when thinking of activities for groups is, 'Is there a point to it?' The rituals I have described work best when they are part of a whole meeting which has a central core or purpose. Tacking on an anointing with oil to the end of a meeting about social justice will only work if people are responding to the challenge of injustice and being anointed to go out and serve God. I have been in a meeting where someone suggested that we all wash each others feet, which we did, but without any understanding of what we were doing other than that it was fun.

If you're going to start from scratch and come up with your own ideas, consider what you are wanting to communicate and think to yourself, 'How would *I* want to respond to that?' An individual response becomes ritualistic or sacramental when you create a channel through which a number of people are helped to share a similar response. The IOU example came from an attempt to encourage a 'professional' suburban church to understand God's claim on their lives. Instead of simply preaching a message, I encouraged a response in which everyone could participate in a meaningful way.

3
MEDITATION AND FANTASY

DEFINITIONS

The human imagination is an amazing thing: we have the ability to know ourselves, to describe our universe and begin to understand it, to use language to evoke imagery and emotions which are uncommon in our daily existence. Why do we have this ability? My head tells me it must be so we can grasp something of the greatness of God. My experience tells me, however, that the church fails to capture or fill my imagination with the things of the Spirit so it ends up being filled with rubbish from the TV, movies and music. When I close my eyes I will often see a TV programme I've been watching or replay a conversation from earlier in the day. If we are indeed to 'take captive every thought to make it obedient to Christ' (2 Corinthians 10:5) that means giving our imaginations a meaty diet of godly imagery. Sometimes what we need is the mental equivalent of a 'detox' diet! This chapter considers the proper use of the imagination in its purest form.

Meditation is a word that has only relatively recently been abandoned by the church because of its connotations with other religions, so I hope to grab it back before it is lost to men in orange robes for good. It just means 'to think deeply'. Until recently, Christian mystics meditated on God's character and even evangelicals were urged to obey Psalm 77:12: 'I will meditate on all your works and consider all your mighty deeds'. Now you can't even mention the word without being accused of selling out to the liberal agenda. No more! We will meditate on the Lord and on his words.

Using the word 'fantasy' is a bit more contentious. I first heard it used in reference to God from the mouth of Sam Richards, now course director at Oxford Youth Works, in about 1991. She used the term 'fantasy journey' to describe something similar to meditation but subtly different: whereas meditation is really about allowing an idea (a Bible verse, for example) to completely occupy your imagination, fantasy journeys put ideas into your head and positively encourage you to take that idea into new realms of... fantasy. I have never experienced the level of imagination that God used in John to visualise the mysteries in the book of Revelation, but you never know, I'm still a beginner! Leading someone through a fantasy journey can have a profound effect on them. I would therefore advise trying one out with a few friends before unleashing this wonderful and powerful technique on an unsuspecting public.

From here on in I am not intending to differentiate too clearly between the two: if you are happy with one and not the other, it will be clear which is which. The key is that we allow the right side of the brain to rule over the left side, just for a few minutes, which gives us a chance to see things differently. If we can't simply package things up into our usual boxes and put them away for further analysis at a later date, we might actually be changed by our experiences. Of all the exercises outlined in this book, I have found fantasy to be the most effective in reaching out to those beyond the church.

SETTING

I have used, and seen used, meditations and fantasy journeys in a myriad of settings. In church services, kids' camps or house groups, taking time out to open the mind to God can be a brilliant starter, main course or dessert to your activities. As you will see, there are some very simple exercises that are brilliant in helping us to tune in to God, some that are quite 'meaty' and take a sizeable chunk of time, and some which allow people simply to reflect on what has already happened in a meeting or over a holiday. However, their use should be governed by your own confidence and ability to handle any fallout.

GUIDELINES

Leading a meditation requires little more than some preparation and enough authority to get everyone to be quiet. Once you have tried the simple exercises listed here, you will be able to develop your own quite easily. You might want to use appropriate music and lighting to allow people to feel at ease: I generally ask people to find a comfortable position, sitting in their chair or even lying on the floor. Don't be in a hurry, leave adequate pauses for reflection and do try to perceive what God might be doing: a period of silence or music at the end of the formal part of the meditation can often be necessary as people continue to deal with issues that God has raised through it.

With fantasy journeys, you need to be much more aware and prepared for anything! As a direct consequence of using fantasy journeys I have had to deal with issues ranging from conversion to secret sins or eating disorders. Therefore if you are planning on using these resources with young people, make sure that you are not the only leader around. Also, pray! Pray before you start the fantasy that God will speak to everyone, and get a couple of friends or leaders to pray while you are leading. Also pray that God will guard the minds and hearts of those taking part.

As you lead a group through a fantasy journey you should be able to pick up what's going on. Normally a few people will not engage with what's going on. Let them know that that's fine but ask them to be quiet so that others aren't distracted. If you see someone becoming distressed, you have a number of options, depending on your own confidence and discernment. You could simply stop the fantasy right there or get a leader to remove the person who is getting upset. Alternatively, you could steer the fantasy away from what you perceive to be causing the distress. Finally, if you feel confident that it is God at work, you can continue with the journey.

An important part of making fantasy journeys effective and positive is how they are begun and ended. I provide two examples of simple exercises that can help a person to 'forget' their surroundings for the period of the fantasy. This is not hypnosis or any other form of mind control: it is to enable us to focus on the job in hand. It is a simple mental technique enabling us to get beyond the usual distracting clutter in our minds. At the end of the fantasy journey, people sometimes need to spend a bit of time 'remembering' where they are or reordering their thoughts. Once this has happened you will need to spend time debriefing, or talking through the exercise. This can be done all together if in a small enough group or in smaller groups of two to four people. Be ready for things to come through the debriefing time.

EXAMPLES

1 In-out (Genesis 2:7; John 20:22,23) ☺

Invite participants to find a comfortable position and to relax. Tell them to close their eyes and focus on their breathing, becoming aware of the sound and feel of the air as it rushes in and out of them. After a while, tell them, as they breathe out, to release any sin or hurt in their lives that they want to give to God, and as they breathe in, to ask for God's forgiveness and the empowering of his Holy Spirit. After an appropriate period of time, advise everyone to become aware of where they are, to move, and then (if appropriate) get them together in groups of 2–3 to pray for anything that God may have brought up.

2 Being there (John 8:1–11) ☺

Read aloud the story of the woman caught in adultery (John 8:1–11). Then ask everyone to close their eyes and imagine that they are one of the characters in the story. You can direct people to particular characters or just let them choose. Retell the story slowly and encourage everyone to work hard at putting themselves into the story. People could be encouraged to notice sights, sounds, even smells! Afterwards, get people to share how they felt or how they viewed things from within the story.

Every word counts (Psalm 119:15; 2 Corinthians 10:5) ☺

Choose any short passage of scripture and take time to focus on every single word. This something probably best done alone, although having someone read out a few words every minute or so can make it a communal experience. The purpose of the exercise is to ask God to speak through deep meditation on the words involved. Allow God to speak to you, explaining the meaning of a passage by giving you words and pictures that will help you understand it.

The Jesus prayer (Mark 10:47)☺

Within the orthodox church, prayers are often chanted. One particular repeated prayer is the Jesus prayer: 'Lord Jesus Christ, have mercy on me.' If you've never prayed like this before, saying or singing a repeated phrase, it can be very strange, but soon you will find that there are benefits. One is that the mind seems to become still while the body continues to pray, so this can be a good exercise to do just for a minute or two before undertaking one of the other exercises.

The blockage (Revelation 1–3)☺

Read Revelation 1–3, picking out some of the different pictures of Jesus in these chapters. Imagine Jesus is standing before you, just a few feet away. Take time to think about the image of Jesus and focus on him. Then ask God to put between you and Jesus, images of anything that is hampering clear communication and a relationship with him. It is then up to you whether you hang on to your rubbish or give it over to Jesus to dispose of. If you can, with his help, hand over all your sinful stuff and then run to him and worship him as you see fit.

You may want to talk through this exercise with a friend afterwards.

A 'forgetting' exercise ☺

To get people ready for a fantasy journey, try this technique. Just say:

'Bring to the front of your mind everything that has occupied your mind today, whether thoughts, or things you have done, or something you have seen or heard. Picture everything right in front of you. (*pause for a few minutes*) Now put all those thoughts into a bottle. Look at them in the bottle: are they all there? (*pause*) Now empty them into a dark container. Watch and check that they all go. Put the container in a cupboard: you'll be coming back for it later.'

This exercise should be taken slowly. When completed, people will have some space in their minds for some imagining! At the end of the meditation/fantasy, you might like to remind everyone to collect their thoughts!

Another 'forgetting' exercise☺

As above, just say:

'Imagine that you are writing to a close friend about today. Write down everything that you've done and everything that you've thought about. Hold nothing back. (*Pause*) Now, fold up the letter and put in an envelope. Take it to the post-box and send it to your friend.'

Move on to a fantasy journey from here.

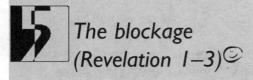

8 The statue (Genesis 1:26–27, Psalm 139) ☺

Get everyone to make themselves comfortable and explain what you're about to do. If you expect feedback afterwards, people need to know that in advance. Say something like this:

'Imagine you are in a large room. In the middle is a statue covered in a large cloth, ready to be unveiled. You go to look at the statue and discover that your name is on its base: it's a statue of you. How does that make you feel? (*pause for a few minutes*) The cloth is now being taken off. Take a good look at your statue. What do you notice? What do you like? What do you not like? (*pause*) Now imagine that you are your statue. How does that feel? (*pause*) Now you notice that Jesus has come into the room. What does he look like? How does he look at you? (*pause*) Now Jesus comes right up to you. You speak to him. What do you say? What does he say back to you? Carry on the conversation for as long as it takes. (*pause*) Jesus then goes away and you are outside your statue again. Look at it again. Do you feel any different about the statue now? (*pause*) Say good-bye to your statue and return to where you are sitting, here and now.'

Give time for people to talk: this fantasy touches on issues of self-image and self-worth and can therefore bring out significant issues, so be sensitive.

9 The heavy load (Matthew 11:28–30) ☺

Get everyone to make themselves comfortable, and ask them to relax and close their eyes. Advise them that you are going to lead them through an imaginative journey and that they will be asked to feed back in pairs at the end of the time. Then guide them through this journey:

'You are in a wilderness. What is it like? What can you see, hear and smell around you? (*pause for few minutes*) You are carrying a rucksack on your back. It is very heavy. Inside it are pictures of all the things that are troubling you: secret sin, other people you are worrying about, etc. Take out the pictures and look at them. (*pause*) Suddenly you become aware of the presence of Jesus with you. You turn around and he is there. What does he look like? What does his face tell you? What does he say? (*pause*) Jesus looks at your pictures and says that he would like to take these things from you. What do you say and do? How do you feel? (*pause*) Jesus is about to leave, and he asks you again if there is anything you would like to hand over to him. What do you say? What do you do? (*pause*) Now Jesus leaves the wilderness and you leave it too, finding yourself back here in the church lounge (*or wherever*). Just spend a minute recalling your journey, and then turn to someone near you and tell as much or as little of it as you like to them.'

Allow ten minutes for a few people to feed back. Then invite any who feel that God has spoken to them to receive prayer from leaders in the group.

10 Friends (Luke 16:19–31; 1 Corinthians 9:19-23) ☺

Prepare people for a fantasy journey as in previous exercises and then say:

'Imagine you are in your favourite place. What is it like? What does it look/sound/smell/feel like? (*pause for a few minutes*) Your best friend or friends are here too. Talk to them. What are you all talking about? (*pause*) Imagine Jesus comes into the room. What does he look like? How does he react to you and your friends? What do you all say to each other? (*pause*) Jesus then turns to go, but before he leaves he turns to you and says, "Will you look after these friends for me?" How do you respond? (*pause*) Now return to where you are and share with someone what God has said to you through the exercise.'

DIY

Writing your own meditations is really about adapting a few ideas to your own circumstances and needs. Adapt the basic methods used above for various Bible or other readings. A fantasy journey will take a little bit more time, but it isn't too difficult once you get the hang of it.

Creating a fantasy journey is about tapping into our common symbolic language. The journey involving a visit to a statue provokes feelings that can be predicted because the images used a common to our daily experience. It feeds on our understanding of ourselves. Even while we are participating in the journey we are aware of deeper meanings. When I first used the 'Friends' journey, I was speaking at a conference about evangelism to young people, and I specifically asked everyone to think of a friend who was not a Christian at the time. This meant that when Jesus came into their special place, they desperately wanted him to be relevant to their friends. As we debriefed, they knew they were struggling not only with their image of Jesus, but also with their friends' image of church.

Start small. A good example of a simple fantasy journey is the meditation on Jesus that I've called 'The blockage'. I wanted to find a way to get people to understand the way sin affects their relationship with God and so I came up with that simple exercise. Moving on from there wasn't too difficult.

One thing to remember is that people will not all respond to a fantasy journey as you do. There can be no way of predicting how certain images or questions will affect someone, so always have a team of folk ready to intervene if the exercise brings up something unexpected. I've never had anything happen in any of the sessions I've led, but I have heard the odd scary story, so it's best to be over-cautious.

4
ROLE-PLAY

DEFINITIONS

On one level, the term 'role-play' is self-defining: it is an exercise in which people take on particular roles. The dictionary definition of role-play is 'an activity in which a person imitates, consciously or unconsciously, a role uncharacteristic of him/herself'. While this definition comes from the world of psychology, we can recognise the core of what we think it's all about.

However, many of us are of a generation (or have children who are) which only hears the term 'role-play' when it's connected to young men with personal hygiene problems pretending to be orcs or dragons or somesuch. The advent of the personal computer has meant that so-called role-playing games (RPGs) occupy a sizeable portion of many a young person's time.

This is not the kind of role-play that I have in mind in this chapter. The purpose of RPGs is to help the player to escape reality and enter a fantasy world, whereas the kind of role-play I am advocating here helps the player to understand the real world better, as well as their own place in it. RPGs provide entertainment, these exercises provide education as well as entertainment.

The advantages of using role-play in teaching are threefold: first, this approach allows you to approach subjects that may be too dry or complex for many groups when taken 'straight'. Second, they provide a personalised empathetic response to a situation, which is much more likely to result in action than the simple passing on of information. Third, they encourage the engagement of *all* group members in the learning process. As you will see below, I have used role-play to educate a group of young people to the point that they take political action on an issue. This can be

satisfying: it is not always the case that young Christians care about child prostitution or the arms trade, although this is normally because they are unaware of the issues.

Perhaps the most vivid example of role-play in the Bible is the marriage of Hosea to Gomer (Hosea 1:2,3). God not only wants Hosea and his family to live as a sign of God's knowledge and anger of their rejection of him, he also wants Hosea to feel and understand the pain and frustration of being a cuckold so that he might communicate it more effectively. Fortunately, we are not often called upon to take such drastic action to understand the heart of God, but perhaps this kind of 'entering into' the heart of the situation is the only way to really understand it. How un-English! Can't we just observe at a distance?

SETTING

Role-play can be an activity which opens people up to emotions they are not used to feeling, expressing or observing. It is therefore vital that a simple role-play like 'Happy families' (below) is set in a wider context, in which people are allowed to speak about those feelings and work through them to a sense of resolution. As you will see, a role-play that touches on aspects of everyday life may well touch on emotions long hidden or forgotten. 'Crisis in the church' can touch on similar intense feelings.

Therefore, I would always recommend using role-plays with some degree of preparation and purpose. When or where depends on the openness and flexibility of your group. I have so far only used role-plays within youth groups and training times where people are ready for something a bit different. I know that after introducing a charity worker to 'Pay-off', she now uses it wherever she goes.

GUIDELINES

Setting is important – you need the right space and environment – but people coming prepared to participate is much more important. Take as much time as you can before the meeting, and before you actually begin the role-play, to encourage everyone to enter into it. You may need to watch out for certain individuals. If you've ever played a murder mystery game at a dinner party, you'll realise that some people are better at getting into role than others!

Your role is vital throughout the game: don't ever be tempted to play! It is vital that everyone playing the game can look to you to tell them what is happening, what they should be doing and what is going to happen next. It is inevitable that even though you explained perfectly how the game was going to played, someone was out at the loo or not listening! You are responsible for briefing, monitoring and debriefing the game; the participants are responsible only for themselves.

Debriefing

The debriefing element of role-play is just as vital as the game itself. Don't take a breather once the game is over. If it has gone well, there will be a number of people beginning to deal with the experience. It is your job to help channel their thoughts and feelings into a constructive outcome: this may be reconciliation, repentance, action or self-awareness. You cannot dictate how someone is going to grow, but you can encourage them to learn.

The best way to debrief is simply to ask people to recount their experience as candidly as they feel able. You may want to ask questions like these:

- What happened in the game, from your perspective? Why did the game take the course it did?
- What were the key turning points in the game? How were decisions made? Were there leaders and followers? Was this a good thing or a bad thing?
- How did you feel during the game? How do you feel now? How do you think others feel?
- Have you learned anything through the game? About yourself? About the others involved? About (whatever the subject of the game is)?
- Do you need to do anything as a result of playing this game? (You could follow up certain role-plays with 'Dear me' (p15)

EXAMPLES

1 Will you just listen? (John 8:43,47; James 1:22–25)

This is a simple idea which I presume is used frequently in conflict resolution situations. If there is an issue about which people in your group disagree, why not set up a debate role-play in which those who take opposing views most strongly are asked to argue (well) the case to 'the opposition'? Give people time to research and prepare their arguments: the best way to do this is to get your debaters together before the meeting and make them listen, in depth, to each other. Then have a simple debate with speakers for and against, and questions from the floor. You may like to encourage *everyone* in the group to take the opposite view to the one they really hold, although this can often lead to complete confusion! I would advise against having winners and losers as the key is to help the main protagonists in the real-life debate understand the thinking behind the views they disagree with. Briefing is important if you do this because it is possible that speakers will fail to do their research and produce merely a parody of the position they disagree with, thus exacerbating the situation.

In the right situation, this role-play can be undertaken by two individuals who have some disagreement, but I would advise that it is undertaken in the controlled context of wider support and/or counselling.

2 Happy families (Deuteronomy 6:4–9; Proverbs 17:6; Ephesians 6:1–4)

This role-play will probably produce a strong reaction in some of the participants. It is supposed to! Its purpose is to make participants aware of the way that family relationships are influenced by 'outside' events and coincidences, and that a failure to talk about them can result in conflict and sadness. This is adapted from a game the origins of which I cannot trace. The total playing time is approximately 45 minutes, including 15 minutes debrief.

Get everyone into groups of 3. Get each group member to take on the name A, B or C, then hand out a copy of the relevant card to each person (see next page), with the instruction that they must not show the card to the other two in the group.

Explain that you are going to enact three short role-plays where each member of the group will have a chance to be a parent, child and observer. In each one it is tea-time and a young child is coming home from school. The observer should watch carefully how the role-play progresses and then feed back her/his observations immediately, taking care to note what feelings are on display and what may or may not be being left unsaid. You may want to spend a few minutes brainstorming on what it's like to be eight years old, to help people get into character before you start. Allow 3 minutes for each role-play and 5 minutes for feedback and discussion after each role-play.

When all three role-plays are completed, bring everyone back together for a more general debrief. The main lessons here are about communication and power, but there will no doubt be other issues raised.

A

Game 1 You are an eight-year-old child coming home from school. You have spent the day in the country on a nature trail, and you are now coming home to tell your parent how great it was.

Game 2 You are a parent waiting for your child to come home from school. An aunt is visiting this evening but you have forgotten to tell your child this. You are very tired and know that the child's presence will keep the aunt occupied.

Game 3 Observer.

B

Game 1 You are a parent waiting for your child to come home from school. You have just lost your job and are deep in thought about how you are going to meet your debts.

Game 2 Observer.

Game 3 You are an eight-year-old child coming home from school. On the way home you witnessed a terrible car accident and have run home in distress to tell your parent what you have seen.

C

Game 1 Observer.

Game 2 You are an eight-year-old child coming home from school. All your friends are going to the cinema this evening with your best friend's parents. You have lied to your friend's parents and said that you had asked permission to go when in fact you forgot to ask. This is a huge treat for you and you must now find a way to ask permission to go.

Game 3 You are a parent waiting for your child to come home from school. Yesterday you asked the child to tidy their room and, as usual, he/she hasn't done anything. You are determined to deal with the issue decisively when the child comes home and listen to no excuses.

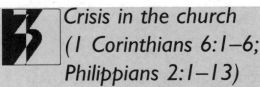

Crisis in the church
(1 Corinthians 6:1–6; Philippians 2:1–13)

This game needs at least 8 players, plus you as leader. It is much better played with large numbers (say 50), but I have adapted it for small-group training on the joys of church youthwork! It simulates a melodramatic crisis precipitated by an enthusiastic church youth group, but deals with a wide variety of issues, including leadership, vision, church in society and more general issues of conflict resolution. You need to divide your participants into a number of teams (preferably so they are not playing themselves):

Church council/PCC/diaconate/ whatever is appropriate (up to 10 players).

The pastoral team (up to 10 players).

The children's and youth team (up to 10 players).

The youth group (about one-fifth of the total number of players).

Church members (no limit).

What you need:
- Everyone needs to hear and/or see the summary of events: my chosen method would be to read out the summary (more dramatic) and then copy it onto an OHP acetate for people to refer back to it when they need to. You could always make a copy for every team member. If you want to add topical details, that's fine: I've done it about coal strikes, green issues and student loans!
- Each group needs a copy of the group briefings.
- There needs to be a copy of the 'special input' for each group.

SUMMARY OF EVENTS

The following is a summary of the events which have led up to the present crisis. These are all generally known to members of the congregation.

SATURDAY

Most of the members of the youth group and a few adult members of the church take part in a protest demonstration involving about 2,000 people. It ends in a violent confrontation with anti-protest forces. About 50 arrests are made, though none of the church people are arrested. Robert Brown (can be Roberta Brown if it becomes a female part), a member of the youth group, is interviewed by a TV reporter. He identifies himself as a member of the church and says that he is taking part in the demonstration because he is a Christian. He goes on to say that the youth group has been studying social and political issues and that the members are convinced that Christians must be involved in radical action to renew society.

SUNDAY

The local Sunday paper gives front-page coverage to the violent confrontation. The youth group is not mentioned.

At the morning service, the minister says that he has received telephone calls from several church members, expressing concern over the church's name being linked with radical action and violence. He makes a plea for understanding and Christian grace on the part of all concerned. The main point of his sermon is the Christian's obligation to stand firm in his convictions.

After the service, a couple of influential church members are observed to ignore the minister's outstretched hand. They go off, apparently angry, without speaking to anyone.

MONDAY

The local paper features an interview with the minister, under the heading, 'RADICAL REVEREND BACKS YOUTH PROTESTERS'.

TUESDAY

The paper prints half a dozen letters commenting on various aspects of the demonstration. One of them criticises the youth group's involvement in the demonstration and also comments on the minister's remarks as reported in Monday's paper.

An editorial in the same paper suggests that communist influence was behind the demonstration.

WEDNESDAY

Overnight the front door of the church has been painted red. Painted on the wall are the words 'FOR COMMUNISTS ONLY'.

Many more letters appear in the paper. They are mainly critical, but two commend the youth group's participation in the demonstration and the backing given by the minister. One of the critical letters is signed by a wealthy member of the church. He identifies himself as a member, but hints that he may withdraw his support if the church 'continues to involve itself in matters which should not concern it'.

News of the church-daubing hits the evening paper and the local TV news. It is reported as 'the price of radical action'.

The church council has called an emergency meeting for tonight to assess the situation. All church members are entitled to be present. Members of the pastoral team, the children's and youth team and the youth group are particularly asked to attend. It is generally anticipated that the youth group will be hauled over the coals. The council will make a decision based on what happens at the meeting. Tomorrow night there will be a meeting of the entire congregation to discuss the matter and to decide where the church goes from here. All members will be entitled to vote at that meeting.

CHURCH COUNCIL

WEDNESDAY

You are meeting to discuss the crisis that has arisen in the church following the youth group's participation in the demonstration last weekend. You have called an emergency meeting for tonight. All church members may attend, but you have specifically asked that members of the pastoral team, the children's and youth team and the youth group be present. You have 15 minutes to prepare an agenda for the meeting and to plan strategy. You will need to appoint a chairman to preside at the meeting. You are responsible for the general functioning of the church and all its organisations. Your main concern is for the good of the church as a whole. Three members of the council are parents of youth group members.

In addition to what is known to all members of the congregation, you have the following information:

1 You have received a copy of a letter sent to the minister by the youth group, thanking him for his support over the demonstration.
2 Several important people in the community (not members of the church) have commented to council members about the situation. They have been critical, apart from one who was 'glad to see the church getting involved in important issues for a change'.
3 Two church members with large pledges have threatened to withdraw their support unless the youth group is disciplined.
4 Rumour: some other members are considering cancelling their pledges/transferring their membership elsewhere.
5 Rumour: it was a member of the youth group who tipped off the TV about the church-daubing this morning.

PASTORAL TEAM

WEDNESDAY

You are meeting to discuss the crisis that has arisen in the church following the youth group's participation in the demonstration last weekend. An emergency meeting of the church council has been called for tonight and you have been asked to attend. You are responsible for assisting the minister in the pastoral oversight of the whole congregation. You also feel a responsibility to function as a support group to the minister. Choose one member of the group to play the role of the minister, the Rev. William Gray. You have 15 minutes in which to discuss the situation and to plan a strategy for tonight's meeting. One member of the committee is the parent of a youth group member who was involved in the demonstration.

In addition to what is known to all members of the congregation, you have the following information:

1 The minister has received many telephone calls and letters from both church members and others, commenting on the situation. About half have been critical, expressing alarm at the way in which the church's name has been linked with the protest movement.

2 The minister has received a letter from the youth group, thanking him for his support over the demonstration, and stating that they are sending a copy to the church council.

3 The minister's wife has had to deal with several anonymous, abusive phone calls. She is having trouble sleeping at night.

4 Several church members are putting pressure on the minister to discipline the youth group and to disown the stand attributed to him in Monday's paper.

5 The report of the interview in Monday's paper is substantially correct, but the minister regrets its headline, which was used without his prior knowledge.

6 Three people have asked to have their names removed from the membership rolls.

THE CHURCH AND YOUTH TEAM

WEDNESDAY

You are meeting to discuss the crisis that has arisen in the church following the youth group's participation in the demonstration last weekend. An emergency meeting of the church council has been called for tonight and you have been asked to attend. You are responsible for the planning and oversight of all the work with children and young people. Since the youth group's participation in the demonstration apparently stems from its study programme, you may come under fire at the meeting. You have 15 minutes in which to discuss the situation and to plan strategy for tonight's meeting. Two members of the team are parents of youth group members who took part in the demonstration. One member of the team was also involved in the demonstration. Assign this role to a member of the group.

In addition to what is known to all members of the congregation, you have the following information:

1 One member of your team took part in the demonstration and is fully in agreement with the stand taken by the young people.
2 Rumour: at least two wealthy and influential church members have threatened to cancel their pledges.
3 The father of one of the girls in the youth group has expressed concern at their study of social and political issues. He demands that this study programme be terminated and that a course of Bible study replace it. He claims to have the support of 'at least half the parents of youth group members'.
4 Robert Brown has told one of your members that the young people are convinced that they are right in this matter, and that they will stand by all they and the minister have said.

THE YOUTH GROUP

WEDNESDAY

You are meeting to discuss the crisis that has arisen in the church following the youth group's participation in the demonstration last weekend. An emergency meeting of the church council has been called for tonight and you have been asked to attend. You anticipate fireworks. You have 15 minutes in which to discuss the situation and to plan strategy for tonight's meeting. You expect to be asked to justify the action taken by the young people last Saturday and the statement made by Robert Brown.

In addition to what is known to all members of the congregation, you have the following information:

1 You have sent a letter to the minister, thanking him for his support in this matter. A copy has been sent to the church council.
2 One of the local TV stations wants to feature the church in a special documentary programme which will explain how and why the youth group has become involved in 'radical action'. The TV people have made an approach through Robert Brown, who suggested that they contact the minister.
3 Robert Brown has received several anonymous phone calls along the lines that the Lord will punish him for his blasphemy and wickedness.
4 Rumour: the children's and youth team are going to stop all youth activities apart from a Bible study programme.
5 One member of the children's and youth team also took part in the demonstration. You believe that s/he is in full agreement with your stand and will support you at the meeting.

CHURCH MEMBERS

WEDNESDAY

You are meeting to discuss the crisis that has arisen in the church following the youth group's participation in the demonstration last weekend. An emergency meeting of the church council has been called for tonight. As church members you are invited to the meeting, but the church council will make a final decision. Some of you are parents of youth group members. Some yourselves took part in the demonstration. You have 15 minutes in which to discuss the situation and to plan strategy for tonight's meeting.

In addition to what is generally known about the situation, the following rumours are circulating:

1 The church council is going to ask for the minister's resignation unless he makes a public statement disowning the stand attributed to him in Monday morning's paper.
2 The minister's wife is on the verge of a nervous breakdown.
3 Several families have left the church because of what has happened.
4 The youth group is going to be closed down.
5 One of the richest members has cancelled his pledge.
6 There has been a threat to burn down the church.

CHANNEL 6

By Hand

The Reverend William Gray
Community Church
Anytown

Dear Mr Gray,

We were in contact earlier today with Robert Brown, a member of your youth group. Robert, of course, is known to us through his participation in the protest demonstration last Saturday. He suggested that we get in touch with you.

In line with our policy of getting behind the news to let the public know what is really happening in our community, we would like to feature your church – and especially its young people – in a 30-minute documentary, with the working title 'Radical Religion.'

We would want coverage of the normal Sunday functions of the church, plus interviews with you, the young people who were involved in the demonstration, and the various officers and leaders of the church. This could be shot this coming weekend with key interviews on Saturday and worship and other activities on Sunday morning, together with some man-in-the-pew comments, with a view to using it the following week.

We need an immediate reply, so we can get things rolling. You will appreciate the haste: your church is news *now*. In a couple of weeks, the world may have forgotten all about you.

Channel 6 would, of course, make a donation to the church's funds in appreciation of your anticipated co-operation.

Yours sincerely,

(signature)

Henry Lawson
Local Documentaries

ROLE-PLAY PROGRAMME (total playing time: 2 hours):

1 Introduction (10 minutes)
2 Group meetings (15 minutes)
3 Meeting of church council (20 minutes)
4 Special input
5 Group meetings (15 minutes)
6 Congregational meeting (30 minutes)
7 Debriefing (30 minutes)

1 You (as leader) outline the purpose of the game. Read or hand out the summary of events. Outline the programme above, but don't mention the special input!

Divide everyone into groups as you choose, but each group needs to have one or two people able to speak out in debate. The church council needs to pick a chairperson, the pastoral team needs to appoint Reverend Gray (who will chair the congregation meeting unless the council decides otherwise), the children's and youth team should choose someone to be the member who was at the demonstration, and the youth group needs to appoint Robert(a) Brown.

Each group moves to its own meeting area. The group briefing sheets are distributed. If you have more than ten in any group, you may want to divide the group up for better discussion. When all groups have received their sheets, announce the beginning of the group meeting period.

2 Group meetings last for 15 minutes. During this time the groups discuss the crisis and decide on strategy for the meeting of the church council. The council also has to draw up an agenda for the meeting, which they need to know is only 20 minutes long!

3 The groups come together for the church council meeting. The chair presides. Anyone can speak, but if any decision is to be made, only the council members are allowed to vote.

Once the 20 minutes is up, announce that the groups all have 15 minutes to prepare for the church meeting, at which final decisions need to be taken. Unless other arrangements have been made, the minister will chair the church meeting, and he and the pastoral team will set the agenda.

4 Hand out the letter from Channel 6 to each group.

5 Groups meet again for 15 minutes. Each group needs to prepare for the coming church congregational meeting.

6 Church meeting. Everyone is permitted to speak and to vote. A decision must be made about all the major items.

7 Debriefing. The whole group looks back over the exercise. Use questions like these:

What decisions were made?
How did people feel at particular points?
Which groups found themselves in conflict with other groups?
Which points became matters of conflict?
What could have happened to change the outcome?
What usually happens when there is conflict in the church?
What kinds of issues are likely to cause conflict?
Ought the church to keep out of conflict situations?

Adapted from *Simulation Games 1* by Pat Baker and Mary Ruth Marshall, (JBCE, Melbourne, 1986). Used by permission of Uniting Education, PO Box 1245, Collingwood 3066, Australia.

4 The housemaids (Matthew 18:1–6)

This game was written as an introduction to the issue of child pornography, but it only works when the participants are unaware of the ultimate subject matter. A group of Thai villagers are basically being invited to sell their daughters into prostitution, which they are unlikely to do unless they are tricked into believing they are selling their daughters to a happier fate.

For this game you need three groups plus two extra 'actors' (ideally male) who will help you lead the game. You will also need some stickers for name tags: Thai names are not too easy to remember!

ROLE-PLAY PROGRAMME (total playing time: 1 hour):

1 Introduction (10 minutes)
2 Village gathering, including meeting with Somchai (5 minutes).
3 Group meetings, including arrival of Butra (25 minutes).
4 Village gathering (5 minutes).
5 Families decide (5 minutes).
6 Conclusion and debrief.

The game:

1 Introduction

Appoint a village council of about 5 people (to be authentic they should all be male). Then get people into groups of about 4–6 people. Within each group they need to 'create' a family with at least one daughter aged between twelve and sixteen. These daughters then form a separate group (returning to their families later in the game).

Hand out the group profiles and give each group time to study them. Then read or hand out the introduction.

2 Village gathering

Call the groups together for the village gathering and have Somchai, one of your actors, ready.

Somchai speaks, either reading out the script provided or improvising on it.

3 Group meetings

There will be another village gathering in 25 minutes at which the council will make its recommendation. The village council must retire and decide what it will recommend. The girls and families go into their groups (all the daughters together, families as individual units) for 10 minutes to talk about the proposals and then the daughters split up and join their families for the remaining 15 minutes. Somchai is free to travel around the groups trying to persuade them to his own point of view.

After about 10 minutes of the discussion, Butra (your second actor) joins the village council. He has advice on what to say.

4 Village gathering

When the 25 minutes is up, the village gathering is reconvened. The council must make its recommendation.

5 Families decide

Each family has 5 minutes to make its own decision.

6 Conclusion and debrief

After each family has reached a decision and explained why it was made, read out the conclusion.

Debriefing should involve some kind of follow-up. Contact Jubilee Campaign (Jubilee Action, St Johns, Cranleigh Road, Wonersh, Guildford GU5 0QX; tel: 01483 894787; email: info@jubileecampaign.demon.co.uk) for more details about child prostitution and how Christians can respond.

GROUP PROFILES

The village council

You are a small group of village elders who are responsible for all matters concerning your village, which is in north-west Thailand. While you do organise everything that happens, you have great authority and so your advice will often be heeded. You are proud of your village and want the families to succeed.

The families

You are a family living in a small village in north-west Thailand. The father and boys in the family farm the small amount of land you have, for rice. The mother and girls look after your small, one-room home. You are generally happy with village life and are glad that the big city has not influenced your part of the country.

The daughters

You are all young teenage girls living in a small village in north-west Thailand. You love your families and help your mothers in the family homes, but village life is boring. To make the game a bit more human, choose a name and create a name-tag so that everyone knows who you are. Thai names include: Orawan, Rattapom, Jantra, Yaminar, Mi Lair.

INTRODUCTION

Your village is just like many others in the furthest corner of Thailand: small, close-knit and poor. But this year, things have been particularly bad. The rains flooded the land, washed away much of the crop and killed many livestock. Everyone in the village will need to borrow money to buy food, but there is no way to pay it back. The weather has meant that a number of the younger children are getting diseases, the medicines for which also cost money. There has been a general air of despair in the village until a man from the nearest town, Chiang Mai, came to the village with an idea for raising funds. This man, named Somchai, is coming back to the village today to explain his plan to a gathering of the whole village.

For Somchai: NOT TO BE SEEN BY ANYONE ELSE!

You are a regional recruiter for a large crime syndicate based in Bangkok. Your job is to recruit young girls to be prostitutes in Bangkok and elsewhere. Your scam is outlined in the script you read or you can improvise on it in the first village gathering:

'Hello! My name is Somchai and I work for a job recruiting company in Chiang Mai. Business is booming and I am here looking for young girls to work as housemaids for the more affluent members of the population of Chiang Mai. The pay is good and the town is not too far away. I appreciate that many of you will not want your daughters to leave the village, but I can assure you that we can make it worth your while. Your daughters will be encouraged to write home at least once a week and they will get a day off once every month to come home and see you. My agency can ensure that you receive part of the girls' earnings, which will go either to individual families or to the village council for distribution. You can be sure that we keep an eye on our girls, so we know what they're doing all the time.'

When the gathering breaks up, you have 25 minutes to go round all the families and the village council to persuade them to agree to your plan. Start with the council, because you have a friend coming to see them soon who will help you with them. His name is Butra and he is an elder from another local village. He knows what you are doing, but the money you are giving him (insignificant to you, enormous to him) makes him your ally. He will authenticate your story to the council, saying that the young women from his village are all on your 'scheme'. Be careful not to stray too far from the material above and try to include a grain of truth: these villagers *will* get some money but they will probably never hear from their daughter again. Teenagers, huh!

If all is not going well, you may like to try suggesting that the village elders might profit personally from a 'commission' on the girls you hire...

For Butra: NOT TO BE SEEN BY ANYONE ELSE!

You are a local village elder who has been recruited by Somchai, whom you know to be a crook obtaining prostitutes for the big cities. However, when he came to your village he 'spared' your own daughters and put you on a fat retainer so you would travel round with him, telling other villages that he is straight. When you arrive you will have 15 minutes to persuade the council that they should support Somchai's proposal. You should play on the fact that you are local and understand their problems, particularly in that they have neither food nor money. Try not to be too fanciful, but explain that there have been benefits in your own village. You can say (honestly) that you see your own daughters regularly!

CONCLUSION

The villages in the north-west of Thailand – the poorest in the country and culturally different from the south where the majority of the population lives – are ripe for picking by the organised crime syndicates which run the brothels in Bangkok and other big cities. Simple folk, the northerners often tend to be so desperate for money that they seem to be willing to suspend judgement and sell their daughters into sexual slavery. Some of them, like Butra, are simply bribed and allow their kinfolk to be abused. Other villages, like your own, are seduced into letting their daughters go. Still others wake in the morning to find the girls have disappeared. If you have seen through Somchai and Butra's plan to corrupt your daughters, you are to be congratulated, except that many, if not all, of your children will now die along with you from starvation and disease. You are the only village in your area which has not benefitted from this minor gold rush: yes, the village would receive some money, even if you never saw your daughters again. But in a few years Somchai will be back, complaining that the girls never write, but what about your next daughter? Would she like to work?

 ## Pay-off (Matthew 6:24; Luke 12:15)

This game teaches, through role-play, both the benefits of co-operation and the dangers of greed. It can create a significant amount of conflict and is best played with a reasonably mature group: when I tried it on a group of eleven to fourteen-year-olds, they went mad!

You will need a 'game director' and 'banker'. Set up 4 teams of equal numbers, far enough apart that each cannot hear the deliberations of the others. You will also need 120 pieces of card or Monopoly money (allow each team to start with 10), and 2 coloured cards for each team (in this case, the colours are red and black: change the rules according to the colours you are using). You will also need a watch with a second hand to record the time. Write out the pay-off formula (below) on one big sheet of card so everyone can see it, or on small cards, one for each team. Then read out the rules.

Pay-off formula

4 reds	Everyone loses 1 chip to the bank.
3 reds, 1 black	Each red wins 1 chip from bank. Black loses 3 chips to bank.
2 reds, 2 blacks	Each red wins 2 chips from bank. Each black loses 2 chips to bank.
1 red, 3 blacks	Red wins three chips from bank. Each black loses 1 chip to bank.
4 blacks	Everyone wins 1 chip from bank.

The rules

1 This game is called 'Pay-off' and the aim is to win as many chips as you can. For each round, the teams choose one of their coloured cards and hold it up. Chips are then awarded/deducted according to the formula.

2 There are ten rounds. The first five will be played without conferring between teams but during the last five rounds conferring will be allowed.

3 You have 1 minute to make your choice during the first five rounds and 2 minutes thereafter. You should keep your choice secret. All teams will then reveal their choices simultaneously.

Run the game and pay out according to the formula. The earlier rounds may need less time and the later ones more, so be flexible.

The catch in this game is that you are telling *everyone together* to maximise their income, not each team, since this can only be achieved through 4 blacks. Count up the total for the *whole group* and compare it with the possible total of 80. There will be fireworks, I promise.

Debrief:

Explain that the score possibilities ranged from 0 (everyone always chose red) to 80 (everyone always chose black). See if anyone was aware of the merits of collaboration and how it affected the way they played the game. This game has led into discussions about Third World poverty, about the nature of sin and about whether we should play competitive games at all! It is also a good teacher in team-building situations, in conjunction with other games.

Adapted from *Simulation Games 1* by Pat Baker and Mary Ruth Marshall, (JBCE, Melbourne, 1986). Used by permission of Uniting Education, PO Box 1245, Collingwood 3066, Australia.

DIY

Writing your own role-plays is a difficult but learnable skill. The key to a good role-play is to lead someone into an experience they might otherwise not have. This works best when the person is unaware of what is coming next and has simply to go along with the flow, in character. However, a role-play like 'The housemaids' works even though a well-read person will know exactly what's coming because s/he is still learning what it's actually like to be in that position.

That role-play was specifically written to introduce a campaign about child prostitution, and this is perhaps a good place to start. You need to think of a dramatic situation to put your characters in, something that will bring out the issues and/or tensions you are wanting to look at. 'Crisis in the church', despite being a full night's work, normally leaves people talking because it gives them a new perspective on something they care about. 'Pay-off', which is a brilliantly devised game more than a role-play proper, gives all the players a new view of themselves...

Think about who the role-play is for. As I mentioned earlier, I completely misjudged an eleven to fourteen-year-old youth group when I tried 'Pay-off' on them. They just weren't able to process the ideas and feelings that the game brought up. Get the right game and you will get the right response: overwhelm and you will get tears; underwhelm and you will get yawns.

Role-plays need to have both purpose and openness. You need to know what the idea behind the game is, but within that subject there is room for the characters to make decisions. It is in making decisions about how the game will develop that learning takes place: the outcome of the game is influenced by me, so I must get involved and not just observe.

You also need to think about how to brief and debrief a situation well, which is just as hard as writing the game itself. Some of the role-plays I've written or used have failed because people have not got into character or understood what's expected of them. Take the time to explain everything and to help people learn from what they have experienced. Otherwise, what's the point?

Finally, keep trying! One of the reasons this chapter only has a few examples is because I'm not willing to share most of my own efforts! However, you can create some great learning experiences through this method with a bit of trial and effort.

5
PLAY

DEFINITIONS

I should own up at this point and say that this chapter is not like any of the others. While I can witter on about the importance of this or that learning method, games are just games and I tend to love them! Most of us know how to play, or at least we used to when we were young. It's not something that has to be explained, exemplified or theologically justified. We have probably all been in situations where someone has used simple play to open up a learning experience. It's like the joke in the sermon: the speaker uses it to get your defences down, then goes for the jugular.

Einstein was quite insistent that 'God doesn't play dice', so that might prove to be a problem to us in this matter (he has since been proved wrong by what has come to be known as 'chaos theory', but that's another story...). We are in fact hard-pressed to find any evidence of games in the Bible. There are no chess matches between Solomon and the Queen of Sheba and no apostolic footie matches (so that's why they got rid of Judas: he was a man too many). However, I think most of see the use of play in a number of settings. Within this chapter I won't be including games that are just mad, stupid and/or fun, although I have absolutely nothing against drinking cola through a sock, etc. It's just that this book is about learning...

SETTING

This is where my headings feel a bit silly. Where is a good place to play? Anywhere you can get away with it, I would suggest. Obviously, most of these games work best within the context of a wider learning experience, but beware of only using games in this way. Only yesterday, I started off a small group meeting with a simple, pleasant get-to-know-you game. When we'd finished, one of the group members asked me what the game had to do with the evening's subject. Talk about conditioning!

GUIDELINES

As the above real-life embarrassment indicates, you can over-use games with meaning so that they lose their punch. Beyond that, the only guidelines you need are those that govern behaviour within your group. By which I mean, can your group handle the idea of people pouring porridge down each others trousers?

EXAMPLES

WARM-UP GAMES

1 Getting to know you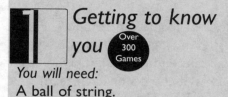

You will need:
A ball of string.

Players sit in a circle. The first player holds the ball of string and introduces himself in two minutes or less, giving his name, job/school, interests, hobbies, etc. Holding the end of the string, he then throws the ball of string across the circle to another player, preferably someone not known to him, and that person introduces herself to the group. Players hold on to the string for the duration of the game. The game continues so that as many participants as possible have an opportunity of sharing. The game ends when the string runs out or an agreed time is completed.

The string criss-crossing is a symbol of friendship and linking together.

TRUST GAMES

Trust games encourage participants to trust one another for their physical safety. This can lead to trusting one another with other things such as hopes, dreams, worries, etc. Trust games may also be used as a lead-in to sessions looking at issues where trust is important (ie friendships, church relationships) or at a particular Bible story where trust was involved.

2 Leaning

Have participants working in groups of 3. They stand in a line with two at either end facing in towards each other, and the volunteer in the middle, facing one of them. The volunteer crosses her arms over her chest and leans forward, keeping her feet in the same place on the floor. The outer person supports her as she 'falls' and gently pushes her back towards the other who is ready to catch and gently support her before pushing her slowly back the other way. The two outer people must concentrate and move slowly so that the person in the middle is always supported and doesn't feel unsafe. The person in the middle must relax but make sure that her feet stay in one place on the floor.

3 Leading the blind

Get participants into pairs. The pair join hands side by side and one closes his eyes. From now on, the game must be conducted in silence. It is the job of the 'seeing' partner to guide his 'blind' partner around the room, avoiding any obstacles and other pairs. Ask the 'blind' person to be thinking about where he is in the room during the journey. When you finish the exercise, bring all the pairs to a halt and ask each 'blind' person, before he opens his eyes, to say where he thinks he is in the room. It's interesting to see how accurate their sense of direction is. Swap over so that the 'blind' partner now becomes the 'seeing' one.

LISTENING GAMES

These games encourage participants to concentrate and listen carefully, filtering out useless sound in order to hear the information they need. You can use them simply as a fun starter game, or to lead in to a session which focuses on a listening-related topic, ie prayer, spending time with God, relating to other people.

Over here

Get participants into pairs: A and B. Position all of the As at one end of the room or playing area and all the Bs at the other. Bs face their partners and close their eyes. On a given signal, As call out to their partners, guiding them towards them, ie 'move forward ... stop ... take one step to the left'. They are not, however, allowed to use their partner's name. Bs concentrate hard in order to hear their partner's voice and filter out the surrounding sound.

Continue until all partners are together again.

Partners swap roles and repeat.

Bosses and secretaries

You will need:
Newspaper cuttings (all of equal length); pencils and paper.

You will need 4–8 players on each team. Half the team are the bosses, the others are their secretaries. Give the newspaper cuttings to the bosses, and a pencil and paper to each secretary. The bosses stand about 4m away from their secretaries, facing them (if space allows). All speaking at the same time, each boss then dictates the contents of the newspaper cutting to their secretary who takes it down. The first pair with a complete record of a reasonably accurate dictation are the winners.

You might like to complicate the game by putting large sweets in the bosses' mouths before they start to dictate.

TEAM GAMES

The following games are useful in encouraging individuals to work as a team, relying on each other or observing each other carefully.

Fire! Fire!

You will need:
Two identical buckets for each team, one filled with water; a supply of plastic cups.

Any number of teams can compete. Each team lines up in single file, with a bucket of water at one end of the line and an empty bucket at the other. Each team member has a cup. The object is to pass the water by transferring it from one cup to another down the line. The team to get the most water into the empty bucket is the winner.

Shoe shucking

You will need:
A washing-up bowl filled with water for each team.

Girls will need to wear trousers or shorts for this game. Divide into teams of 6. Team members lie on their backs, with their feet in the air and touching in the centre of a circle. Place the container of water on their elevated feet. The team then works together to allow each team member to remove their shoes without spilling any water. The winning team is the one with the most shoes off after 4 minutes.

Group juggle

This is hard to explain but once you've got it, it's great fun. Take one ball and throw it around a circle of about 10 people. Each person must receive the ball once *and only once*, remembering who has already had the ball, before it finally comes back to the person who first threw it. You then repeat the process, always throwing to the same person and slowly adding more balls until it ends in madness. When it works well this game can instil a good sense of non-competitive teamwork.

THEME GAMES

Often you can use simple variations on well-known games to supplement your teaching material. The importance is in the application – what you do with it – and the discussion and thinking time afterwards.

 ## Across the gap

This game can be played indoors or outdoors. For the indoor version the jumping will have to be done from a standing start on the edge of the string; whereas if played outdoors there can be a run-up before jumping.

You will need:
Two lengths of rope or string; four chairs.

To play:
Tie the lengths of rope or string to the bottoms of the chair legs so that you have two parallel lengths of stretched-out rope. The rope should be flat on the ground. The gap between the ropes should be fairly narrow to start with – maybe a metre. The aim of the game is for the players to jump over the ropes, completely clearing the gap in the middle.

If you have a large group, you may like to divide them into 2–3 teams and have one member from each team run and jump simultaneously, provided the ropes are long enough. Otherwise play it as a simple turn-by-turn jump off. When everyone has jumped the original gap, move one pair of chairs and rope further away, thus widening the gap, and have a second jump off.

More and more players will be eliminated each time the gap is widened. Finally, make the gap so wide that not even your champion jumper can clear it.

Theme points – Jesus the way / sin.
See John 14:6, 'I am the way, the truth, and the life; no one goes to the Father except by me.' This game ties in with Jesus being the only way to the Father. We cannot reach God by our efforts alone: there is a gulf separating us from God – like the gap the children tried to jump. We can try to jump the gap by all sorts of methods (being 'good', saying our prayers, trying all sorts of other religions, going to church) but none of them work! We will fall in the gap (which is caused by sin) and we need Jesus to bridge the gap for us.

You can illustrate this by putting a line of chairs across your gap and saying that now anyone can cross – no need to jump – and everyone will be a winner. Through Jesus we can all 'win' the race and reach God.

© Lesley Pinchbeck. Adapted from *Theme Games* (Scripture Union 1993)

 ## Noises off (John 10:14–16)

You will need:
Pencils and paper; either a large, empty box or a curtain plus noise-making equipment, or a tape of pre-recorded noises plus a cassette recorder. Making your own tape of sound effects need not be difficult. Noises to record could include:

A paper bag bursting
Water running from a tap
A door closing
Keys jangling
Footsteps
Water boiling in a kettle
A book being shut quickly
Newspaper rustling
Milk bottles clinking together
Someone eating crisps

Make a list of noises as you record them so that you can identify them later! Leave short gaps between your sound effects.

Alternatively, you could rig up a curtain or use a large cardboard box as a screen behind which to make some of the noises listed above. In this instance you will need more 'transportable' noises such as:

Cutting paper with scissors
Pouring water into a glass
Opening a packet of crisps
Striking a match

Either give everyone a pencil and paper, or divide them into groups and give each group a piece of paper and a pencil. Tell them that you have made a tape of 'noises off' but you have forgotten what they are. You will play it and see if they can identify them for you.

Play the tape, pausing briefly between each sound effect so that they have enough time to write down what they think they've heard. Don't pause too long, keep it moving and tell them to have a guess at it if they're not sure.

When you have finished, rewind the tape and go through it again, asking the group to tell you what they thought they were hearing for each sound. If you chose to play in groups, they can score points for each correct answer.

Theme points – discernment / hearing / listening / discernment / blindness and sight. Listening is a major part of this game. Listening carefully and not being distracted by those around you – this is how we should listen to God. Discernment also comes into it here, how do we tell noises apart? How do we tell God's voice from other, misleading voices? What is discernment? It is telling things apart.

Blindness is a related theme – it is not so easy to identify things if we cannot see as well as hear, and spiritual blindness can be brought into this. And we need to see God at work as well as hear his voice. God gave us our senses – he gives us the ability to see and hear him as well.

© Lesley Pinchbeck. Adapted from *Theme Games* (Scripture Union 1993)

 ## Police!

You will need:
Large assortment of brightly coloured and 'silly' clothing, eg odd socks, two different shoes (one boot, one slipper), a silly hat (shower cap?), scarf, gloves (different colours!), shorts (to be worn outside trousers). Have accessories too, eg sunglasses, bright red lipstick (use on nose if you like for painted-on freckles), a wig, umbrella, balloons, teddy.

A volunteer leader dresses up beforehand in all this silly gear, but *none* of the group must get a glimpse – this is important!

To play
Have the whole group sitting in a circle and announce to them that before you begin, you have something rather important to tell them. You then go on to say something along these lines:

'There was a robbery last night at my house, someone's pinched all my best clothes! He even took my teddy bear! I shall have to call the POLICE!' As you get to the word 'police', shout it out loud, and your accomplice should burst in, run round the group – shrieking and cackling like a maniac – and zoom out of the door again. (Your accomplice should remain outside for a moment longer.)

Into the stunned silence (?) you now say, 'That was him! Quick – write down a description for the police!' At this point have the group divide into two teams who must then compile as comprehensive a list as possible of the suspect's appearance within a given time limit – three minutes or so. Alternatively, you can have a master list pinned up and ask the group to tell you what the suspect was wearing and write it up yourself.

At the end of the time limit, say that you will now call the POLICE! At this signal your accomplice should run back into the room and this time stand at the front with you while you check off which group had the fullest, most accurate list

– or what it was that they didn't remember from your master list.

Theme points – day of the Lord / Jesus' return / God knows us
You can use the shock effect of this game to draw parallels with the idea that 'the day of the Lord will come as a thief comes at night' (1 Thessalonians 5:2). What effect did it have? It took you by surprise, so much so that it was hard to think straight. This is what Jesus was warning us about – we should be prepared for his unexpected return.

You may like to use this game to link with other observation type games, to point out that God knows everything about us – 'every hair on your head is numbered' – right down to the colour of our socks! And nothing about us is unimportant to him.

© Lesley Pinchbeck. Adapted from *Theme Games* (Scripture Union 1993)

12 Blindfold breakfast (2 Corinthians 4:4)

You will need:
For each team you need a bar of chocolate on a plate; knife and fork; die and throwing cup; scarf for blindfold; a pair of gloves.

To play
For each team, put a plate with a bar of chocolate and a knife and fork on a chair or table on the opposite side of the room to the players. Give each team a die, throwing cup, blindfold and pair of gloves. It is a good idea to have a referee available to check that the blindfolds are securely tied as required.

The teams commence play, passing their dice round and trying to throw a six. When a player throws a six, he has to put the gloves on and allow the other team members to blindfold him. He is now turned round three times, then the team must direct him to the chocolate without touching him at all. Once he has found the table, the team tell him where to put his hands to find the knife and fork, and where to aim with the knife and fork to cut the chocolate, spear a piece on the fork and eat it.

The winning team is the first one to feed their blind man a square of chocolate. Share the remaining chocolate between the team members.

Theme points – blindness and sight / caring / helping / trusting
Ask the blindfolded players how it felt. Did they keep wanting to peer round the edges of the blindfold? It is frustrating not being able to use your eyes – as well as difficult. Jesus talked about blindness and he also healed the blind. What sorts of blindness does the Bible mention? What is 'spiritual blindness'? Your blind man was able to have breakfast because the team rallied round to help. We are told to help our less able brothers and sisters. We can easily imagine being blind simply by being blindfolded temporarily. It's not so easy to sympathise with people with other problems, such as depression, stress or hidden worries, but we should try to be aware of them and to help them too. This game also illustrates trusting – the blindfolded player had to trust the others to lead him safely. We can trust Jesus to lead us safely and keep us safe.

© Lesley Pinchbeck. Adapted from *Theme Games* (Scripture Union 1993)

Over 300 Games

Games taken from *Over 300 games for all occasions*, compiled by Patrick Goodland (Scripture Union 1998).

THEMATIC INDEX

INDEX OF BIBLE PASSAGES

(VERY) SELECT BIBLIOGRAPHY

Creativity
There are a number of academic books on the subject of creativity, but I have yet to find a practical manual. Dean Borgman's *When Kumbaya is not Enough* (Peabody: Hendrickson 1997) has a few good chapters about this but still nothing too practical.

Ritual and Sacrament
There are obviously lots of books that look at these subjects from a more traditional standpoint. Pete Ward's *Youth Culture and the Gospel* (Marshall Pickering 1993), while lightweight, does begin to ask the right questions and describe some efforts to answer them. Sadly it's now out of print but a good browse in a bookshop may turn up a copy. Failing that you may be able to borrow someone else's.

If you have access to the internet you might like to check out http://www.greenbelt.org.uklaltgrps/altgrps.html

Meditation and Fantasy
Anthony de Mello's *Sadhana* (Doubleday US 1978) is a modern classic and I have also found *God in All Things* by John Callanan helpful (Doubleday US 1993). *God of Surprises* by Gerard Hughes (Darton, Longman & Todd Ltd 1985) is wonderful for personal devotion, as is *Godzone* by Mike Riddell (Lion Publishing 1992).

Role-Play
If you are lucky you might be able to get hold of any of the four *Simulation Games* books published by JBCE in Melbourne, Australia. Two of their games have been adapted in the chapter on Role-play. I've not seen anything quite like them.

Play
Many of the best games books are published by Youth Specialities in the US: you can often get a catalogue from your local Christian bookshop. If you are completely mad, have a look at Pip Wilson's books (all Marshall Pickering).

Over 300 Games for All Occasions compiled by Patrick Goodland (Scripture Union 1993) is an invaluable handbook for anyone involved with children or young people and *Theme Games* by Lesley Pinchbeck (Scripture Union 1993) is a comprehensive resource-book of games through which young people can learn, grasp concepts and take ideas on board. It contains over 150 games arranged thematically, and is well-indexed.

'Get a Life'

and other sketches for your youth group

Want to spice up your youth events with creative and original drama?

This collection of fifteen funny, hard-hitting and, frankly, quite brilliant sketches explores a range of topical issues, from getting your head round the concept of faith, to findng out what real freedom is all about. Written for all levels of experience, this lively collection will prove a valuable and exciting resource for youth groups of all kinds.

- ❤ 'Do-able dramas' with handy tips on props and performance.
- ❤ A broad range of styles and approaches to suit your needs.
- ❤ Includes discussion starters for use afterwards.

ISBN 1 85999 232 3

Price £6.99

**Available from your local Christian bookshop or
from Scripture Union, PO Box 764, Oxford, OX4 5FJ
Tel: 01865 716880 Fax: 01865 715152
(Please add £3.00 p&p for mail order.)**

A photocopiable resource